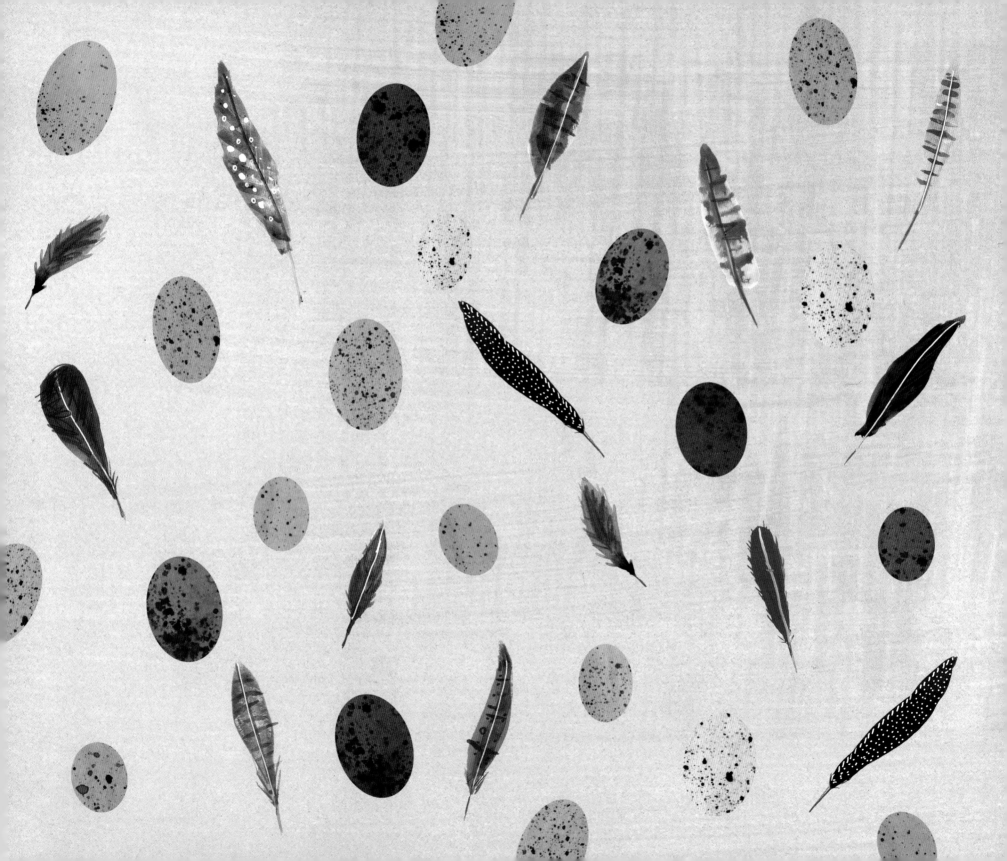

BIRD GIRL

Gene Stratton-Porter

Shares Her Love of Nature with the World

Written by **Jill Esbaum**
Illustrated by **Rebecca Gibbon**

CALKINS CREEK

AN IMPRINT OF ASTRA BOOKS FOR YOUNG READERS

New York

Wabash County, Indiana, 1871

On the Stratton farm, everybody pitches in to keep things running smoothly.
Even seven-year-old Geneva Grace gathers eggs each morning.
But as soon as she's finished in the stuffy chicken coop . . .

. . . Geneva is free to roam.

All the farm is hers to explore, and she wants to try *everything*.

Who cares if her apron tears or her face and hands get scratched up?

Whatever else Geneva is doing, she's always watching birds and wondering . . .

How do they decide where to build their nests?

What do they feed their babies?

Does all that chirping and singing *mean* anything?

She's been watching a hawk family for weeks . . .
and worrying. If Father finds out these predators live
so close to the farm's chickens, there'll be trouble.

So, every day Geneva picks up anything
the hawks have pushed from their nest,
anything that might give away their
location. Into the brook she tosses the
bones of rabbits, ground squirrels, and . . .
uh-oh, chickens.

But one day she hears a gunshot—*crack!*—and
sees a hawk whirling to the ground.
She jumps between her father and the bird.

"Oh, Father, please don't kill him! . . .

. . . Give him to me!"

In two days, Geneva has the hawk
drinking water from a bowl and eating
meat scraps from the end of a stick.

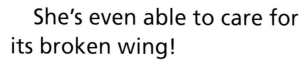

She's even able to care for
its broken wing!

From then on, the family delivers any injured
bird straight to Geneva.
Most fly away healthy and whole.

Others stick around awhile—
like Hezekiah, the blue jay she
teaches to roll a cherry across
the ground.

The next spring, itching to do more for her beloved birds, Geneva takes on the care of sixty-four nests. She visits each one every day, inching forward softly, silently, watching and wondering.

If a bird so much as twitches a wing,
she freezes . . . and waits for it to relax.

The birds, wary at first, are soon chirping
hellos and flitting onto Geneva's head and
shoulders, tiny claws tickle poking, as she pulls
treats from her apron pocket.

Happy birds, happy bird girl.

Geneva is eleven years old when her father retires and moves the family to a nearby town.

Everything here feels wrong.

The house is too small and has no yard. School is too hard, especially math. Geneva feels like a faded bumpkin next to the town girls.

Then her mother dies, and the girl's world is upended yet again.

Her only bright spot is caring for the nine
caged birds she brought from the farm.

Slowly, the bird girl adjusts to town life.
But she never stops longing for the country.

In the Spring of 1895, Geneva is a grown-up married lady—now called Gene—when she finally moves back to the country.
She can hardly wait to renew her special relationship with birds.

That's why her conservatory windows have special hatches. When they're open, feathered friends can fly in and out as they please!

At long last, the time feels right for Gene to pursue her secret dream—writing about birds. Not made-up tales, but true stories of her own experiences.

But when a magazine wants to pair her true stories with drawings of stuffed birds, posed in silly positions that look nothing like living birds . . . Gene feels her dream slipping away.

No, thanks, she says.

Months later, daughter Jeannette's parrot, Major, is acting up at the dinner table. He isn't satisfied with the coffee-dipped cracker Jeannette gives him. No, he clearly wants the oyster stew the family is eating.

The girl fishes an oyster from her bowl. When Major gobbles it greedily and begs for another, Gene laughs and says, "How I wish I had a camera!"

Guess what she gets for Christmas?

Her first photo is of Major. It's blurry and streaked. Yet it has Gene running through the house, shouting for joy. *This* is how she'll illustrate her bird stories!

Well . . . that's *if* she can teach herself to take better pictures.

By spring, Gene is raring to go. She packs a buggy with all the equipment she'll need and rolls into Limberlost Swamp, an oozy, overgrown wilderness less than a mile from her back door.

She remembers everything she learned as a little bird girl. That's why she . . .

. . . wears dull colors to keep from frightening the birds.

. . . knows where to find nests.

. . . inches forward softly, silently, to set up her camera.

If her subject so much as twitches a wing, Gene freezes . . . and waits for it to relax.

Gene turns the family bathroom into a darkroom.
Her first photos are disappointing.
Okay, so this isn't going to be as easy as she'd
hoped. But practice makes perfect, so . . .

. . . back to the Limberlost she goes.
There's nothing Gene won't do for a great shot.
Who cares if her skirt tears or her face and hands get scratched up?

For fourteen days in a row, she sloshes through murky, hip-deep swamp water, holding high her forty-pound camera . . .

. . . to get the perfect close-up of a nesting rail.

She hangs upside down over a muddy bank to peek into a kingfisher's deep, fragile tunnel nest.

Anybody in there?
Well, hello!

She fights through
spongy muck and
tangled undergrowth—
rattlesnake territory—to reach
the hollow tree where a
vulture nests. She goes back
time and again to capture the
world's first photo series
of a growing vulture chick.

After five years of roaming the Limberlost, of watching and wondering, of capturing on film thousands of catbirds and cardinals, orioles and owls, finches and thrushes and cuckoos and hummingbirds and warblers and more, Gene has not only rediscovered her childhood love for birds, but now knows more about their behavior than just about anybody.

Bird Woman of the Limberlost. That's what folks start calling her.

Gene has also rediscovered the boundless and bone-deep love of nature she knew as a child. Every blooming, buzzing, chirping, croaking, fluttering bit of it. Let it go? Never again. But she'll happily share it with the world.

Recreation magazine's editor pulls prints from an envelope and can hardly believe his eyes.

These are living birds—in their natural habitats, in photos so close-up and clear he can count the feathers!

Gene Stratton-Porter.
Who is this woman?

Just a curious farm girl who fell in love with birds

and watched

and wondered.

AUTHOR'S NOTE

Geneva Stratton, ten years old, 1873

Gene Stratton-Porter was one of America's first bird photographers and became one of the most famous authors and naturalists of her time. Her books were wildly popular across America and around the world. By 1924, ten million of them had been sold, and many were made into movies.

All of Gene's books, whether nonfiction or fiction, included plenty of what she sometimes called "nature stuff." That nature stuff is what kept readers coming back. Thousands of them wrote letters to tell her so. They often added that her books had sparked in them a commitment to protect wild places. That was Gene's proudest accomplishment. She knew what happened when nature's wild places were lost. She'd seen it outside her own back door.

By 1910, there wasn't much left of her beloved Limberlost Swamp. She'd been watching for years as timber harvesters bulldozed roads to reach its ancient, majestic trees; as oil companies drilled wells to get at underground gas and oil; as farmers funneled swamp water to the Wabash River to create cropland. It was all perfectly legal. Progress, some called it. To Gene, it was reckless and wasteful. Tragic, too, for the creatures who lost their homes.

So, imagine how she would feel to learn that two Indiana conservation groups, inspired by her life and books, began in the 1990s to buy up chunks of farmland and woodsy patches that were once part of the 13,000-acre Limberlost Swamp. Their goal? To bring it back. As of this book's publication, nearly 1,800 acres have been restored.

Native plants and flowers have returned. So have deer, beavers, and otters. Insects are plentiful—including dragonflies, bees, moths, and butterflies. Turtles and frogs paddle plop through marshy shallows.

Buzzing and trilling and croaking fill the air . . . along with the calls and songs of cardinals, blue jays, purple martins, herons, and dozens of other bird species.

That's a happy ending not even Gene Stratton-Porter could have dreamed up.

MORE ABOUT GENE STRATTON-PORTER

Gene Stratton-Porter at her California home, 1924

Gene Stratton-Porter (GSP) was a woman of astonishingly diverse talents. She was an author, photographer, and naturalist, yes. But she was also an in-demand speaker, an artist, a musician, a fisherman, a magazine editor and columnist, a gardener, and more. Here are a few additional facts about this remarkable woman.

• In the late 1800s and early 1900s, young women were supposed to act dainty and delicate. When GSP was twenty years old, she and her sister vacationed at a lakeside resort. "I was considered an outcast, half-demented," Gene later said, "because I fished in the rain one night when I might have attended a ball."

• Once, GSP needed owl photos for a magazine article. But the evening before her deadline, she hadn't yet found an owl. Then she heard a screech owl's call coming from her orchard. She lit a candle in her kitchen, then turned off every other light, opened a window, and crouched beneath. She listened carefully to the owl's calls, then copied them herself. When the owl flew in and perched on a chair, even she was shocked. She took pictures all the next day, then let it fly out.

• GSP really did allow birds to fly inside her house. Moths, too. Here's how daughter Jeannette described their everyday life in a book she wrote about her mother, *The Lady of the Limberlost*:

I was accustomed to all sorts of birds and little animals and insects in the house. Almost any place in our house you might find a glass turned down over a little patch of moth eggs on a rug to protect them; you might find a little strip of paper pinned on a window curtain to protect another moth; you might find a wounded bird, which was being doctored, perched almost anywhere; you might find several different size boxes containing baby caterpillars just hatched, feeding on the particular kind of leaves which they ate; you might find cocoons pinned almost anywhere, and newly emerged moths and butterflies flying through the house and feeding on the flowers in the conservatory. There were little saucers of honey and sweetened water and dampened lumps of sugar placed in different spots for their food.

• Critics often disliked GSP's books. They said her main characters were too nice, too wholesome to be believable. One called *Laddie* "molasses fiction." Her feisty reply to that was, "What a wonderful compliment! All the world loves sweets."

• GSP's books made her wealthy, but she never wanted to stop learning. So she still spent most days out exploring nature, studying birds and moths and anything else that caught her eye.

• In 1914, discouraged by the Limberlost's destruction and the fact that more and more of her fans were showing up at her home uninvited, the Porters moved to a more remote home they'd built on Sylvan Lake near Rome City, Indiana. GSP called

Barn owl, photo by Gene Stratton-Porter

it Wildflower Woods. While living there, she worked hard to gather one of every kind of tree, vine, shrub, and wildflower native to Indiana and replant them on her property.

• While living at Wildflower Woods, a law was passed in GSP's new county that would have allowed the same kind of drainage that destroyed the Limberlost Swamp. She fought against it, and the law was reversed in 1920.

• After a few years at Wildflower Woods, the Porters moved to Southern California. Gene thought the climate would be better for her health. She loved this new environment, especially its unique bird and flower species.

• Gene Stratton-Porter died in a car accident in December of 1924 at the age of sixty-one—just before moving into a mansion she'd had built in Bel-Air, with lavish grounds she designed to be a bird and wildflower sanctuary.

For information about Gene Stratton-Porter and her Indiana homes, visit these websites:

The Limberlost State Historic Site (Limberlost Cabin)
indianamuseum.org/historic-sites/limberlost

Gene Stratton-Porter State Historic Site (Wildflower Woods)
indianamuseum.org/historic-sites/gene-stratton-porter

BIBLIOGRAPHY

The quotations used in the book can be found in the following sources marked with an asterisk (*).

PRIMARY SOURCES

*Stratton-Porter, Gene. *Gene Stratton-Porter: A Little Story of Her Life and Work*. 1915. Reprint. Cabin John, MD: Wildside Press, 2009.

*———. *Homing with the Birds: The History of a Lifetime of Personal Experience with the Birds*. 1919. Reprint, with contributions by Kenneth L. Brunswick. Geneva, Indiana: 48HrBooks, 2019.

———. *What I Have Done with Birds*. 1907. Reprint, with contributions by Kenneth L. Brunswick. Indianapolis: Bobbs-Merrill Company Publishers, 2017.

SECONDARY SOURCES

Brunswick, Kenneth L. *The Limberlost "Born Again": A Lifetime to Restore Gene Stratton-Porter's Limberlost*. Self-published, 48HrBooks, 2017.

Finney, Jan Dearmin. *The Natural Wonder, Surviving Photographs of the Great Limberlost Swamp by Gene Stratton-Porter*. Indianapolis: Indiana State Museum, 1985.

Long, Judith Reick. *Gene Stratton-Porter: Novelist and Naturalist*. Indianapolis: Indiana Historical Society, 1990.

*Meehan, Jeannette Porter. *The Lady of the Limberlost: The Life and Letters of Gene Stratton-Porter*. Garden City, NY: Doubleday Doran, 1928.

Morrow, Barbara Olenyik. *Nature's Storyteller: The Life of Gene Stratton-Porter*. Indianapolis: Indiana Historical Society Press, 2016.

SELECTED WORKS BY GENE STRATTON-PORTER

FICTION

The Song of the Cardinal, 1903
Freckles, 1904
At the Foot of the Rainbow, 1907
A Girl of the Limberlost, 1909
The Harvester, 1911
Laddie, 1913
Michael O'Halloran, 1915
A Daughter of the Land, 1918
The White Flag, 1923
The Keeper of the Bees, 1925
The Magic Garden, 1927

NATURE STUDIES

What I Have Done with Birds, 1907
Birds of the Bible, 1909
Music of the Wild, 1910
Moths of the Limberlost, 1912
Friends in Feathers, 1917
Homing with the Birds, 1919
Wings, 1923
Tales You Won't Believe, 1925

ACKNOWLEDGMENT

Special thanks to Curt Burnette, naturalist/program developer at the Limberlost State Historic Site, for his invaluable assistance.

TEXT CREDITS

For Bria —*JE*

Believe in yourself, you can do it. —*RG*

PICTURE CREDITS

Indiana State Museum and Historic Sites: 36; Indiana
Historical Society, P0391: 37; Gene Stratton-Porter,
University of California Libraries: 38.

Calkins Creek
An imprint of Astra Books for Young Readers,
a division of Astra Publishing House
astrapublishinghouse.com
Printed in China

ISBN: 978-1-63592-686-6 (hc)
ISBN: 978-1-63592-687-3 (eBook)
Library of Congress Control Number: 2023905050

First edition
10 9 8 7 6 5 4 3 2 1

Design by Barbara Grzeslo
The text is set in Frutiger LT Std.
The illustrations are done in acrylic ink and colored pencil.